WEEKLY WR READER®

EARLY LEARNING LIBRARY

**Animals That Live
in the Mountains**

Elk

by JoAnn Early Macken

Reading consultant: Susan Nations, M.Ed.,
author/literacy coach/
consultant in literacy development

Please visit our web site at: www.earlyliteracy.cc
For a free color catalog describing Weekly Reader® Early Learning Library's list
of high-quality books, call 1-877-445-5824 (USA) or 1-800-387-3178 (Canada).
Weekly Reader® Early Learning Library's fax: (414) 336-0164.

Library of Congress Cataloging-in-Publication Data

Macken, JoAnn Early, 1953-
    Elk / by JoAnn Early Macken.
       p. cm. — (Animals that live in the mountains)
    Includes bibliographical references and index.
    ISBN 0-8368-6318-6 (lib. bdg.)
    ISBN 0-8368-6325-9 (softcover)
    1. Elk—Juvenile literature. I. Title.
  QL737.U55M253   2006
  599.65'7—dc22   2005027924

This edition first published in 2006 by
Weekly Reader® Early Learning Library
A Member of the WRC Media Family of Companies
330 West Olive Street, Suite 100
Milwaukee, WI 53212 USA

Copyright © 2006 by Weekly Reader® Early Learning Library

Managing editor: Valerie J. Weber
Art direction: Tammy West
Cover design and page layout: Kami Strunsee
Picture research: Diane Laska-Swanke

Picture credits: Cover, pp. 5, 7, 9, 19 © Tom and Pat Leeson; p. 11 © Susan Day/Daybreak
Imagery; pp. 13, 17, 21 © Michael H. Francis; p. 15 © Jeff Milton/Daybreak Imagery

Printed in the United States of America

1 2 3 4 5 6 7 8 9 10 09 08 07 06

Note to Educators and Parents

Reading is such an exciting adventure for young children! They are beginning to integrate their oral language skills with written language. To encourage children along the path to early literacy, books must be colorful, engaging, and interesting; they should invite the young reader to explore both the print and the pictures.

Animals That Live in the Mountains is a new series designed to help children read about creatures that make their homes in high places. Each book describes a different mountain animal's life cycle, behavior, and habitat.

Each book is specially designed to support the young reader in the reading process. The familiar topics are appealing to young children and invite them to read — and reread — again and again. The full-color photographs and enhanced text further support the student during the reading process.

In addition to serving as wonderful picture books in schools, libraries, homes, and other places where children learn to love reading, these books are specifically intended to be read within an instructional guided reading group. This small group setting allows beginning readers to work with a fluent adult model as they make meaning from the text. After children develop fluency with the text and content, the book can be read independently. Children and adults alike will find these books supportive, engaging, and fun!

— Susan Nations, M.Ed., author, literacy coach,
and consultant in literacy development

A young elk is a **calf**. A female elk is a **cow**, and a male elk is a **bull**. A calf has white spots in its coat. The spots make it hard to see.

Elk are mammals. Calves
drink milk from their mothers.
In about a week, the calves
can run. A few weeks later,
they start to eat grass.

Elk are larger than deer.

They are smaller than moose.

Like deer and moose, they

have hooves on their feet.

Elk stay in groups called **herds**. An older cow leads a herd. One elk watches for danger.

11

Elk use their noses, ears, and eyes to sense danger. They see things that move. They watch out for bears and cougars.

Elk eat grass and other plants. They swallow their food quickly. Later, they bring it up and chew it again.

Bulls have antlers. They **shed**, or lose, their antlers each winter. In spring, new antlers grow.

antlers

In spring, elk move up the mountain. They look for fresh grass to eat. In fall, they move down to warmer places.

In winter, elk grow thick coats to keep warm. They dig through snow to find food. They may eat bark and twigs. In spring, they **molt**, or shed their thick coats.

21

Glossary

antlers — the branched horns of animals in the deer family

danger — a thing that may cause harm or pain

hooves — hard coverings on animals' feet

mammals — animals that give birth to live babies and feed them milk. Most mammals have hair or fur.

swallow — to pass through the mouth to the stomach while eating

For More Information

Books

Deer, Moose, Elk and Caribou. Deborah Hodge
(Kids Can Press)

Elk. Emilie U. Lepthien (Children's Press)

Elk. Scott Wrobel (Smart Apple Media)

Irish Elk. Prehistoric Animals (series).
Michael P. Goecke (ABDO)

Web Sites

Elk
*www.eparks.org/wildlife_protection/
wildlife_facts/elk.asp*
Elk facts and photos

Index

About the Author

JoAnn Early Macken is the author of two rhyming picture books, *Sing-Along Song* and *Cats on Judy*, and more than eighty nonfiction books for children. Her poems have appeared in several children's magazines. A graduate of the M.F.A. in Writing for Children and Young Adults Program at Vermont College, she lives in Wisconsin with her husband and their two sons.